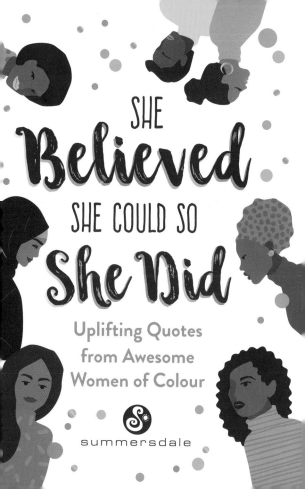

SHE
Believed
SHE COULD SO
She Did

**Uplifting Quotes
from Awesome
Women of Colour**

summersdale

SHE BELIEVED SHE COULD SO SHE DID

Compiled by Sunny Fungcap
Consultant Editor: Candi Williams
Cover design in collaboration with Kelci J

An Hachette UK Company
www.hachette.co.uk

Summersdale Publishers Ltd
Part of Octopus Publishing Group Limited
Carmelite House
50 Victoria Embankment
LONDON
EC4Y 0DZ
UK

www.summersdale.com

Printed and bound in the Czech Republic

ISBN: 978-1-78783-971-7

Substantial discounts on bulk quantities of Summersdale books are available to corporations, professional associations and other organizations. For details contact general enquiries: telephone: +44 (0) 1243 771107 or email: enquiries@summersdale.com.

Fryn Prnnrtt

TO _Ella Pannett_

FROM _Deborah & Ian Morris_

I'M NOT USUALLY A FOLLOWER OF TRENDS. I LIKE TO SET THEM.

PRIYANKA CHOPRA JONAS

THEY'LL TELL YOU
YOU'RE TOO LOUD, THAT
YOU NEED TO WAIT YOUR
TURN AND ASK THE RIGHT
PEOPLE FOR PERMISSION.
DO IT ANYWAY.

ALEXANDRIA
OCASIO-CORTEZ

If you expect to
be happy, you
will always find
something to be
happy about.

DON'T TRY TO FIT IN. STAND OUT. STAND STRONG.

DIANDRA FORREST

You may be the first
to do many things,
but make sure you
are not the last.

KAMALA HARRIS

WE HAVE
TO STEP UP
AS WOMEN
AND TAKE

the lead.

BEYONCÉ

NEVER LET
ANYONE MAKE
YOU FEEL
INSIGNIFICANT.

I GO TO THE PAST
FOR RESEARCH. I NEED
TO KNOW WHAT CAME
BEFORE SO I CAN
BREAK THE RULES.

VERA WANG

I don't know what's next, and I like that idea.

SASHA LANE

Be excited and ready for the unfamiliar.

I'm standing
here to tell you:
you are not alone.
Your tribe of
people, they are out
there in the world.
Waiting for you.

SHONDA RHIMES

I WANT TO EMBRACE MY FULL SELF, AS NATURAL AS I CAN BE.

WILLOW SMITH

MY ADVICE TO WOMEN
IN GENERAL: EVEN IF
YOU'RE DOING A NINE-
TO-FIVE JOB, TREAT
YOURSELF LIKE A BOSS.

NICKI MINAJ

AN EMPOWERED LADY IS A CLASSY ONE.

IT'S IMPORTANT TO KNOW THAT YOU HAVE A COMMUNITY OF GIRLS AND WOMEN SUPPORTING YOU. I AM ONE OF THOSE PEOPLE!

YARA SHAHIDI

If you enjoy
the process, it's
your dream...
If you are enduring
the process, just
desperate for the
result, it's somebody
else's dream.

SALMA HAYEK

If you can
imagine
it, you're
halfway
there.

THE ONLY WAY
TO GET WHAT
YOU REALLY
WANT IS TO LET
GO OF WHAT YOU
don't want.

IYANLA VANZANT

I HAVE A PERSONALITY
DEFECT WHERE I SORT OF
REFUSE TO SEE MYSELF
AS AN UNDERDOG.

MINDY KALING

I believe that telling our stories, first to ourselves and then to one another and the world, is a revolutionary act.

JANET MOCK

CHALLENGES ARE OPPORTUNITIES IN DISGUISE.

You can never
leave footprints
that last if you are
always walking
on tiptoe.

LEYMAH GBOWEE

**EVERY GIRL,
NO MATTER
WHERE SHE LIVES,
DESERVES THE
OPPORTUNITY
TO DEVELOP THE
PROMISE INSIDE
OF HER.**

MICHELLE OBAMA

Be the
change
you want
to see.

I WASN'T WHAT IRANIAN SOCIETY WANTED ME TO BE – A GOOD GIRL. I PLAYED WITH THE LION'S TAIL.

GOLSHIFTEH FARAHANI

YOU HAVE TO TREAT YOURSELF. LIFE IS TOO SHORT TO DEPRIVE YOURSELF OF THINGS.

NATHALIE EMMANUEL

Women don't need
to find a voice.
They have a voice.
They need to feel
empowered to use it
and people need to be
encouraged to listen.

MEGHAN,
DUCHESS OF SUSSEX

BE YOUR OWN CHEER CAPTAIN.

I LOVE FINDING THINGS THAT SCARE ME AND DOING THEM. THAT'S HOW *you grow.*

VANESSA HUDGENS

IT IS REVOLUTIONARY
FOR ANY TRANS PERSON
TO CHOOSE TO BE
SEEN AND VISIBLE IN A
WORLD THAT TELLS US
WE SHOULD NOT EXIST.

LAVERNE COX

Sometimes
encouragement
is a silent voice
telling you to
never give up.

If I'm here I better
do something good.

TAMMY DUCKWORTH

I'm not the next
Usain Bolt or Michael
Phelps. I'm the first
Simone Biles.

SIMONE BILES

DON'T BE AFRAID TO TAKE RISKS. IN RISKS WILL COME YOUR BIGGEST OPPORTUNITIES.

KIRTHIGA REDDY

SUCCESS DEPENDS ON HOW IN LOVE YOU ARE WITH THE JOURNEY.

I'LL NEVER FORGET
WHERE I'M FROM.
IT'S ESSENTIAL TO REMAIN
HUMBLE AND EVOLVING.

FREIDA PINTO

ONE CHILD, ONE TEACHER, ONE BOOK, ONE PEN CAN CHANGE THE WORLD.

MALALA YOUSAFZAI

Confidence isn't about knowing that people like you. Confidence is knowing you'll be fine if they don't.

Your world is only as small as you make it.

GABRIELLE UNION

THERE IS NOTHING
NEGATIVE ABOUT A
GROUP OF PEOPLE
CRYING OUT FOR
DEMOCRACY –
AND IF MY VOICE
COUNTS I WILL
be vocal.

SHIRIN NESHAT

YOU'RE A BAWSE NOW,
AND YOU NEED TO SPEND
LESS ENERGY STALKING
YOUR EX ON INSTAGRAM
AND MORE ENERGY
MAKING PHENOMENAL
FIRST IMPRESSIONS.

LILLY SINGH

NEEDING PERMISSION TO SHINE IS LIKE NEEDING PERMISSION TO BREATHE.

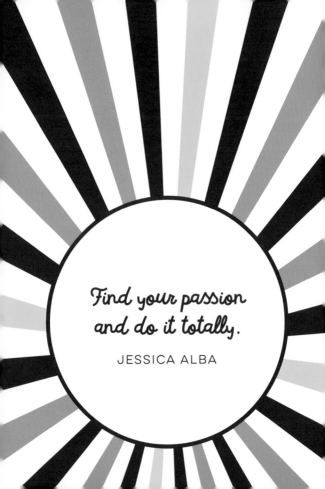

Find your passion and do it totally.

JESSICA ALBA

Truly, truly
love yourself
enough to be your
own best friend,
because you're stuck
with yourself until
the day you die.

MAITREYI
RAMAKRISHNAN

The company
you attract
reflects what
you think you
deserve.

YOU CAN BE THE LEAD IN YOUR OWN LIFE.

KERRY WASHINGTON

CONFIDENT PEOPLE HAVE A WAY OF CARRYING THEMSELVES THAT MAKES OTHERS MORE ATTRACTED TO THEM.

SOFIA VERGARA

OUR ABILITY TO LAUGH DIRECTLY COINCIDES WITH OUR ABILITY TO FIGHT. IF WE MAKE FUN OF IT, WE CAN TRANSCEND IT.

MARGARET CHO

DON'T QUIT TWO MINUTES BEFORE THE MIRACLE.

No matter
where you're from,
your dreams
are valid.

LUPITA NYONG'O

I TRY TO LIVE IN
A LITTLE BIT OF
my own joy
AND NOT LET
PEOPLE STEAL
IT OR TAKE IT.

HODA KOTB

Be a creator and have fun with it.

THE PEOPLE WHO
PUT YOU DOWN DON'T
HAVE TO STOP YOU
FROM CHASING YOUR
DREAMS. STAND UP AND
PROVE THEM WRONG.

SELENA GOMEZ

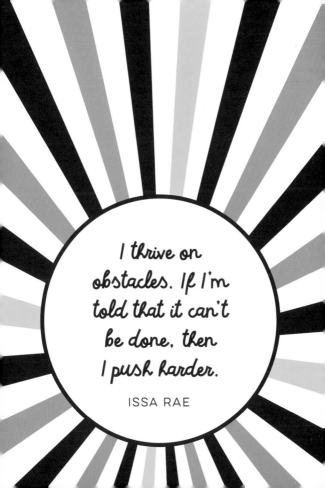

I thrive on obstacles. If I'm told that it can't be done, then I push harder.

ISSA RAE

Normal is nothing more than a cycle on a washing machine.

WHOOPI GOLDBERG

THE WORLD WAS ALWAYS THIS COLOURFUL, ONLY NOW YOU SEE.

I'VE ALWAYS LIKED
TO GO DOWN A
DIFFERENT PATH.
BEING A WOMAN
OF COLOUR,
I NEVER FOLLOWED
A COOKIE-CUTTER
WAY.

HALLE BERRY

WHEN I HAVE
TO MAKE DECISIONS,
I ALWAYS CHOOSE
HONESTY AND
I ALWAYS STAY
TRUE TO MYSELF.

LIZZO

A woman is fifty shades of colour with no make-up.

I DON'T MEASURE MYSELF BY OTHERS' EXPECTATIONS OR LET OTHERS DEFINE MY WORTH.

SONIA SOTOMAYOR

Don't block your blessings. Don't let doubt stop you from getting where you want to be.

JENNIFER HUDSON

EVERY DAY,
I define myself.
I KNOW WHO I AM
TODAY. I DON'T
PROMISE YOU
ANYTHING FOR
TOMORROW.

SALMA HAYEK

YOU ARE
CREATING YOUR
OWN REALITY,
SO BE CLEAR
ON WHAT YOU
ASK FOR.

DON'T WORRY
ABOUT SOCIETY'S
CONDITIONING AND THE
LABELS THAT ARE PUT
ON YOU BY EXTERNAL
FORCES. HOLD ON TO
YOUR TRUE SELF.

GUGU MBATHA-RAW

I love the quote "fail fast" because the greatest lessons are born out of failures and mistakes.

MORGAN DEBAUN

In life we
can become
masters at
being the
students.

**Never stop
believing
in yourself,
you're worth it.**

SERENA WILLIAMS

CREATE
THE HIGHEST,
GRANDEST VISION
POSSIBLE FOR
YOUR LIFE,
BECAUSE YOU
BECOME WHAT
YOU BELIEVE.

OPRAH WINFREY

I KNEW THAT THERE
WAS NO TURNING BACK.
BUT I HAD NOTHING
TO LOSE, AND THAT'S
WHEN THE BEST
THINGS HAPPEN.

AWKWAFINA

NEVER APOLOGIZE FOR BEING YOUR OWN MORAL COMPASS.

I DON'T BELIEVE IN LUCK. IT'S PERSISTENCE, HARD WORK AND NOT FORGETTING YOUR DREAM.

JANET JACKSON

Work hard.
Be so good they
can't ignore you.

GINA RODRIGUEZ

What you
do has a
more lasting
impression
than what
you say.

IF YOU
FOCUS MORE
ON THE INSIDE,
you'll feel
just as great
ABOUT THE
OUTSIDE.

KEKE PALMER

FIND A TYPE OF
EXERCISE THAT YOU
LOVE - WHETHER
IT'S DANCE, SOCCER,
SOFTBALL, ANYTHING
- JUST AS LONG AS IT
KEEPS YOU ACTIVE.

FRANCIA RAISA

Why do you want to fit inside a glass slipper when you can shatter the glass ceiling?

PRIYANKA CHOPRA JONAS

YOU DON'T
NEED TO BE A
TRENDSETTER
TO BE A
TRAILBLAZER.
BE A LEADER.

My body,
my clothes and
my make-up are
on purpose, just as
I am on purpose.

JANET MOCK

BE COLOUR

BRAVE.

MELLODY HOBSON

Something
we all have
in common
is that we
are unique.

I AM SMART,
I AM TALENTED,
I TAKE ADVANTAGE OF
THE OPPORTUNITIES THAT
COME MY WAY AND I WORK
REALLY, REALLY HARD.
DON'T CALL ME LUCKY.
CALL ME A *BADASS*.

SHONDA RHIMES

I'M REALLY EXCITED ABOUT THIS GENERATION OF YOUNG WOMEN THAT CAN LOOK AT A SCREEN AND SEE SOME BROWN PEOPLE IN SPACE.

TESSA THOMPSON

We all start somewhere. It's where you end up that counts.

RIHANNA

INSPIRED ACTION IS ALL YOU NEED TO DO IT RIGHT THE FIRST TIME.

YOU SHOULD
NEVER FEEL
AFRAID TO
BECOME A PIECE
OF ART. IT'S
exhilarating.

NICKI MINAJ

I AM LEARNING EVERY
DAY TO ALLOW THE
SPACE BETWEEN WHERE
I AM AND WHERE I WANT
TO BE TO INSPIRE ME
AND NOT TERRIFY ME.

TRACEE ELLIS ROSS

Be authentic.

Loving yourself
is a process and
everybody's on
their own clock.

ZENDAYA

Sometimes you
just have to put on
lip gloss and pretend
to be psyched.

MINDY KALING

IF YOU ARE ALWAYS TRYING TO BE NORMAL, YOU WILL NEVER KNOW HOW AMAZING YOU CAN BE.

MAYA ANGELOU

THE BEST GIFTS COME IN COLOURFUL PACKAGES.

FOR ME, THE POSSIBILITY IS WHAT DRIVES ME.

ALICIA GARZA

WE CAN PUT FEAR OF THE FUTURE IN FRONT OF US TO BLOCK US, OR BEHIND US TO DRIVE US FORWARD.

MICHAELA COEL

One person
can start a
movement;
together we
can build a
community.

For women,
a lot of the
time, there's that
sense that we
have to work
twice as hard.

NAOMI SCOTT

IF YOUR
DREAM ONLY
INCLUDES YOU,

it's too

small.

AVA DuVERNAY

AN EMPRESS DOES NOT
CONCERN HERSELF WITH
THE ANTICS OF FOOLS.

GABRIELLE UNION

ACKNOWLEDGE AND EMBRACE YOUR DIFFERENCES. IT'S TOTALLY OKAY TO BE DIFFERENT.

The world makes you something that you're not, but you know inside what you are.

GEENA ROCERO

I'm strong,
I'm tough, I still
wear my eyeliner.

LISA LESLIE

We are not
meant to stay
the same.
Choose to
keep learning.

BEING A STRONG, FEARLESS WOMAN MAKES ME FEEL BEAUTIFUL.

LAILA ALI

I'M DRAWN TO PEOPLE
WHO'VE GOT PASSION,
WHO'VE GOT THEIR
BIGGER PICTURE.

TARAJI P. HENSON

I SAY THAT THE MOST LIBERATING THING ABOUT BEAUTY IS REALIZING THAT YOU ARE THE BEHOLDER.

SALMA HAYEK

IMAGINE THE TRIP BEFORE GOING ON THE JOURNEY.

One of the things
my parents taught
me, and I'll always
be grateful as
a gift, is to not
ever let anybody
else define me.

WILMA MANKILLER

WHAT REALLY
FULFILLS ME
IS GETTING
OUT OF MY
COMFORT ZONE,

taking

chances.

HALLE BERRY

Your right
and left feet
don't move
in unison,
but they still
move forward
together.

MY BREAKTHROUGH
CAME WHEN I STOPPED
FEELING SORRY FOR
MYSELF AND TOOK
RESPONSIBILITY FOR
EVERY PART OF MY LIFE.

MARY J. BLIGE

You're going to hear a lot of "nos" before you hear a "yes", but learn to enjoy the process and embrace it.

JAMIE CHUNG

You have to
treat people with
the same respect,
whether they're
signing your cheques
or cleaning up
after you.

RAVEN-SYMONÉ

QUEENS MAKE CHOICES.

GLAMOUR IS ABOUT FEELING GOOD IN YOUR OWN SKIN.

ZOE SALDANA

THE SUCCESS OF EVERY WOMAN SHOULD BE THE INSPIRATION TO ANOTHER.

SERENA WILLIAMS

Own who
you are.

THE ONLY WAY YOU CAN SUSTAIN A PERMANENT CHANGE IS TO CREATE A NEW WAY OF THINKING, ACTING AND BEING.

JENNIFER HUDSON

If I could change
my appearance,
I would have the gap
between my front
teeth put back in.

THANDIE NEWTON

I WANT TO BE

strong

AND EMPOWERED.
I WANT TO SHOCK
EVERYBODY.

VANESSA HUDGENS

BE, FEEL,
THINK AND
SHOWCASE
THE BEST
VERSION
OF YOU.

YOU'VE GOT TO
BE OKAY ON YOUR
OWN BEFORE YOU
CAN BE OKAY WITH
SOMEBODY ELSE.

JENNIFER LOPEZ

If you celebrate your uniqueness then others will too.

DIANDRA FORREST

The best relationships never make you feel like you've lost yourself, but that you can finally be free.

Your life is
your story and
the adventure
ahead of you is the
journey to fulfill
your own purpose
and potential.

KERRY WASHINGTON

REMAIN A LIFELONG STUDENT. DON'T LOSE THAT CURIOSITY.

INDRA NOOYI

MY THEORY IS THAT IF
YOU LOOK CONFIDENT YOU
CAN PULL OFF ANYTHING —
EVEN IF YOU HAVE NO CLUE
WHAT YOU'RE DOING.

JESSICA ALBA

DREAM.
PLAN.
DO.

THE MINUTE YOU LEARN TO LOVE YOURSELF, YOU WON'T WANT TO BE ANYONE ELSE.

RIHANNA

Sometimes the most powerful thing you can say is "no" and not feel the need to do everything. It's about doing what rings true to me.

AMERICA FERRERA

Be brave
and fearless.

You are never stronger... THAN WHEN YOU LAND ON THE OTHER SIDE OF DESPAIR.

ZADIE SMITH

IT'S BETTER TO
LOOK AHEAD AND
PREPARE THAN
TO LOOK BACK
AND REGRET.

JACKIE JOYNER-KERSEE

I think most people are quirky — they're just afraid to show it.

CARLA HALL

CLEAR YOUR MIND AND VISUALIZE EVERYTHING YOU WANT.

The second
you accept
yourself is the
second everybody
else around you
does as well.

GINA RODRIGUEZ

FOR US TO HAVE SELF-ESTEEM IS TRULY AN ACT OF REVOLUTION, AND OUR REVOLUTION IS LONG OVERDUE

MARGARET CHO

Just like
the sunrise,
there is always
another chance
to start again
or start new.

BE STINGY WITH YOUR TIME AND SPEND IT IN SPACES THAT FILL YOU UP.

JANET MOCK

I'D ASK MYSELF,
"DO YOU WANT TO
GIVE UP BECAUSE
IT'S NOT EASY?"

JISOO

We need girls
to know that strong
is beautiful, and to
get them participating
and doing their best,
whatever they do.

ALLYSON FELIX

CHANGING YOUR PERSPECTIVE CAN INSTANTLY CHANGE YOUR WORLD.

I LIKE BEING
A FUNNY LADY.
I THINK THERE'S

nothing
sexier

THAN A
FUNNY LADY.

MAYA RUDOLPH

I'D RATHER REGRET THE
RISKS THAT DIDN'T WORK
OUT THAN THE CHANCES
I DIDN'T TAKE AT ALL.

SIMONE BILES

Celebrate what makes you, you.

After every storm, if you look hard enough, a rainbow appears.

MARIAH CAREY

I truly believe
that the privilege
of a lifetime is
being who you are.

VIOLA DAVIS

THE SOLUTION
HAS ALWAYS BEEN
THAT IT'S UP TO
US TO SUPPORT,
PROMOTE AND
CREATE THE
IMAGES THAT WE
WANT TO SEE.

ISSA RAE

OPPORTUNITIES CAN COME IN THE MOST UNLIKELY FORMS.

WOMEN ARE BEAUTIFUL AND INTELLECTUAL AND SPIRITUAL AND SOCIAL AND ENTREPRENEURIAL. THEY'RE EVERYTHING.

EVA LONGORIA

"WHY AM I HERE?"
IF YOU CAN ANSWER
THAT QUESTION,
YOU'LL BE ABLE
TO DUST YOURSELF
OFF AND SHINE
LIKE A PHOENIX
OUT OF ASHES.

MICHELLE RODRIGUEZ

Whether alone or in a crowd, when you are comfortable with yourself, you are always in good company.

I don't promote
giving up.
I promote fighting
and winning.

NICKI MINAJ

YOU ARE
BEAUTIFUL:
EMBRACE IT.
YOU ARE
INTELLIGENT:
EMBRACE IT.
YOU ARE POWERFUL:
embrace it.

MICHAELA COEL

WHEN LIFE GIVES YOU
LEMONS DON'T MAKE
LEMONADE, MAKE PINK
LEMONADE. BE UNIQUE.

WANDA SYKES

THERE IS ONLY
ONE YOU AND
ONLY ONE
LIFETIME TO
MAKE THE
BEST VERSION
OF YOU.

There's no better make-up than self-confidence.

SHAKIRA

**Take my little
light and shine
it in darkness.**

LEYMAH GBOWEE

IF YOU'RE INTERESTED IN FINDING
OUT MORE ABOUT OUR BOOKS, FIND US ON
FACEBOOK AT SUMMERSDALE PUBLISHERS AND
FOLLOW US ON TWITTER AT @SUMMERSDALE.

WWW.SUMMERSDALE.COM

IMAGE CREDITS

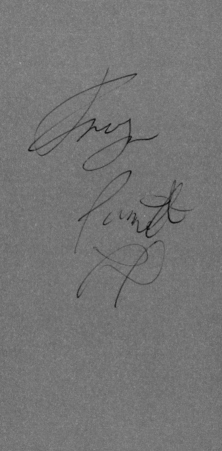